# Animal Helpers

Heather Hammonds

## Contents

Rigby

A Harcourt Achieve Imprint

www.Rigby.com
1-800-531-5015

# Pets

It is fun to have a **pet**.

You can play with a pet.

You can look after it.

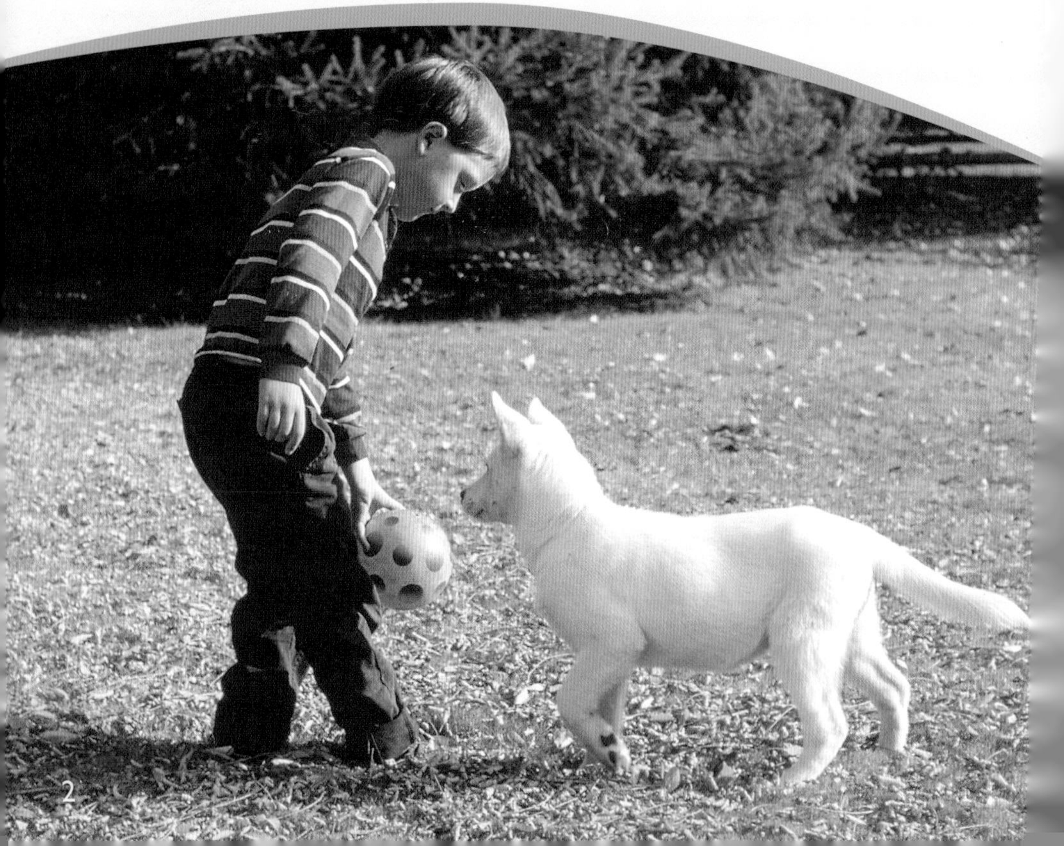

Some animals are not pets.

They are animal helpers.

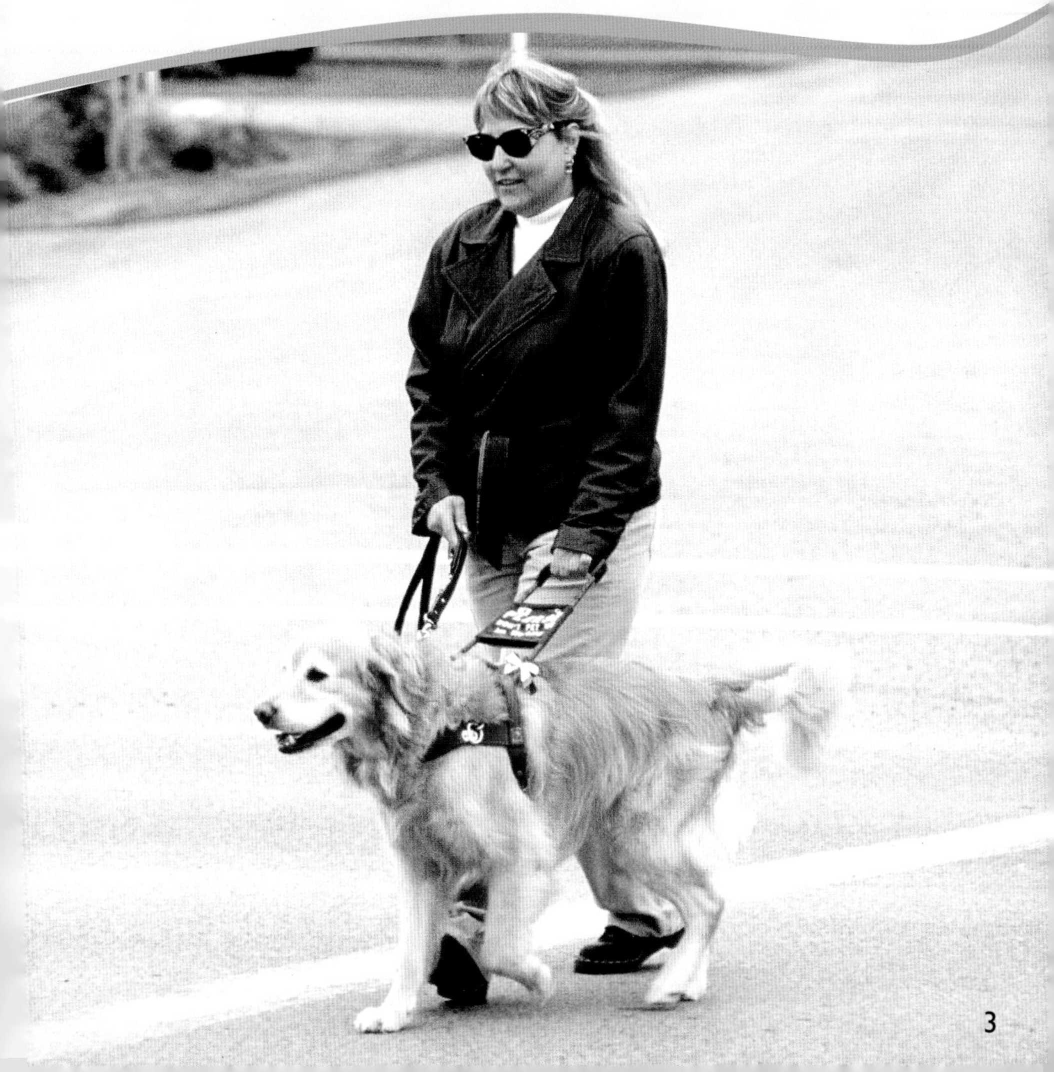

# Dogs

This dog helps the man go for a walk.
The man cannot see.

The dog can see if it is safe to cross the road.

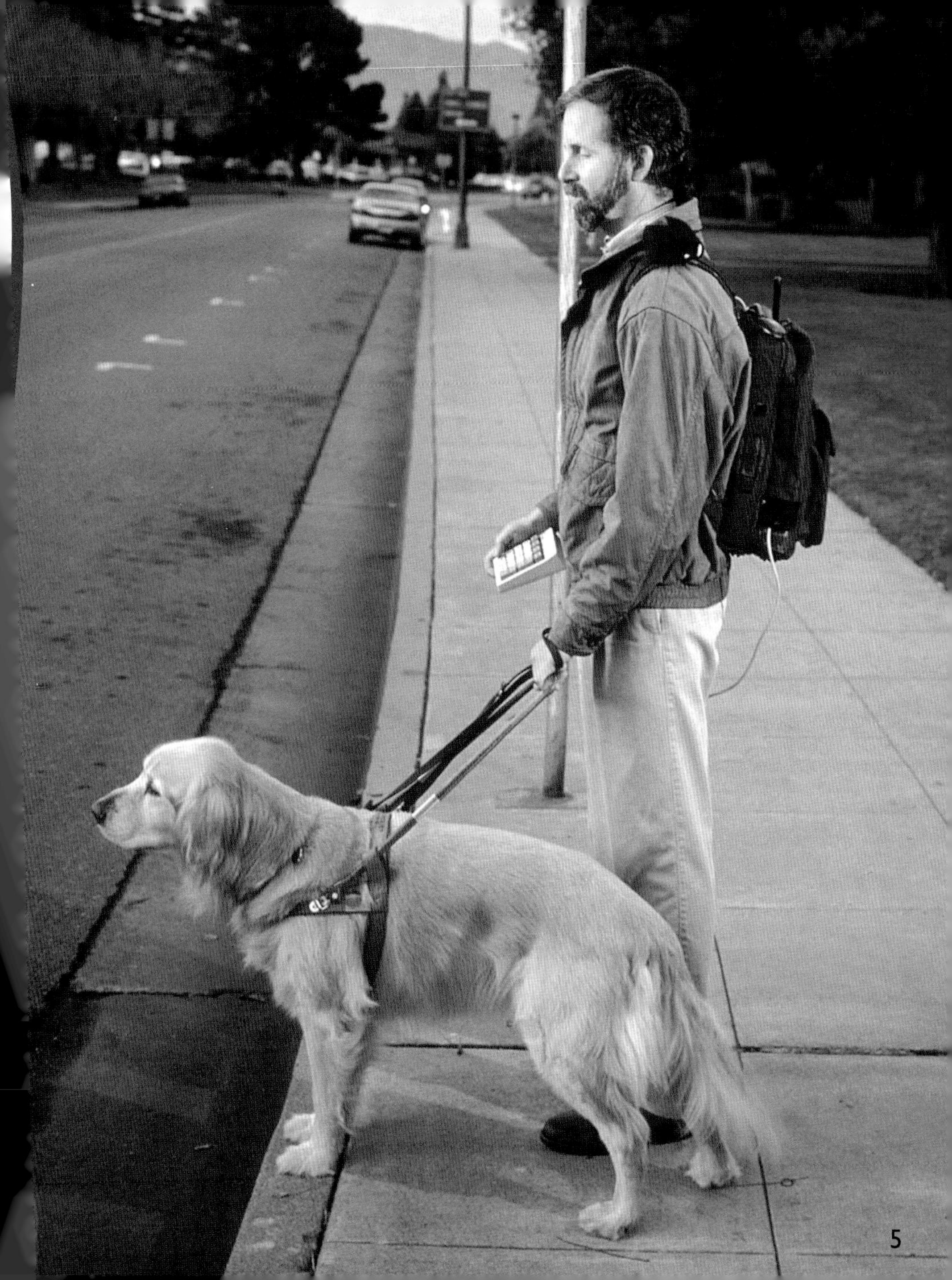

This dog helps the **farmer** look after the sheep on the farm.

The dog can run very fast!

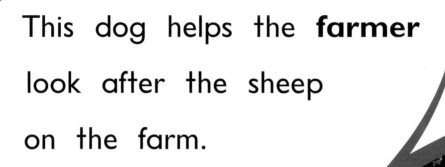

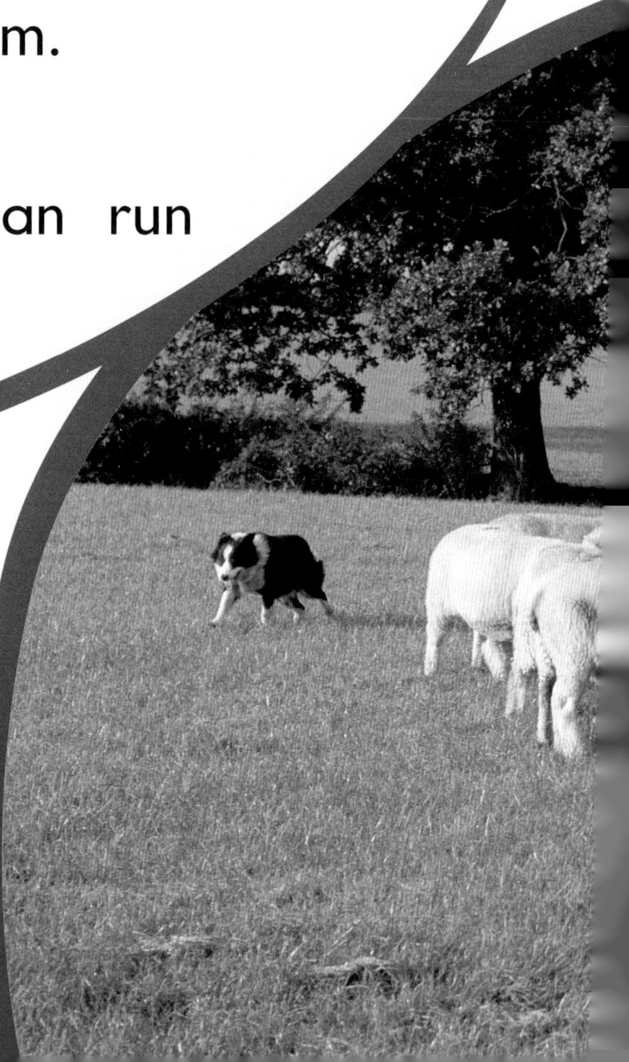

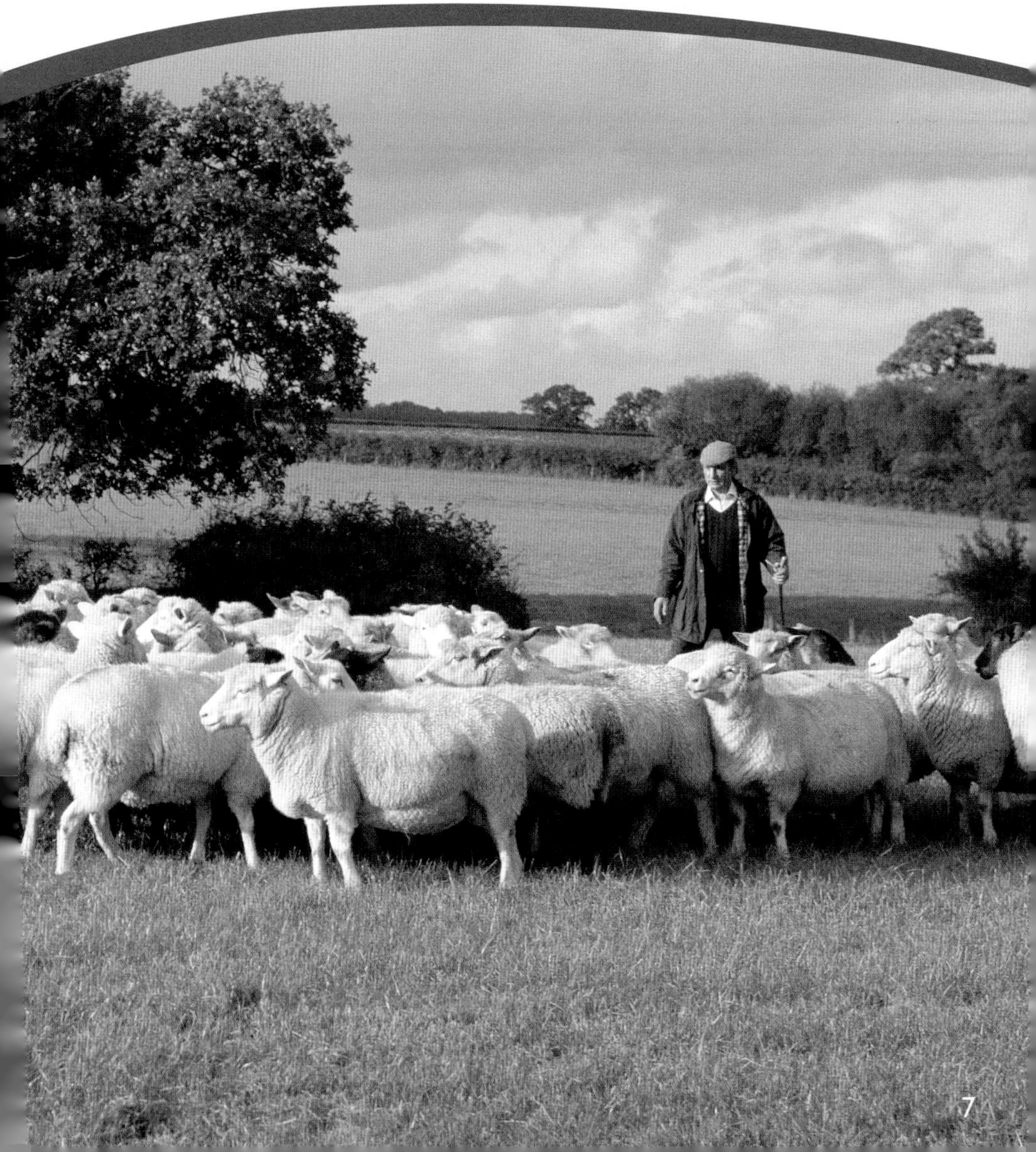

Look at this big dog.

The big dog is very brave.

He stays by the **policeman**.

He helps the policeman
with his job.

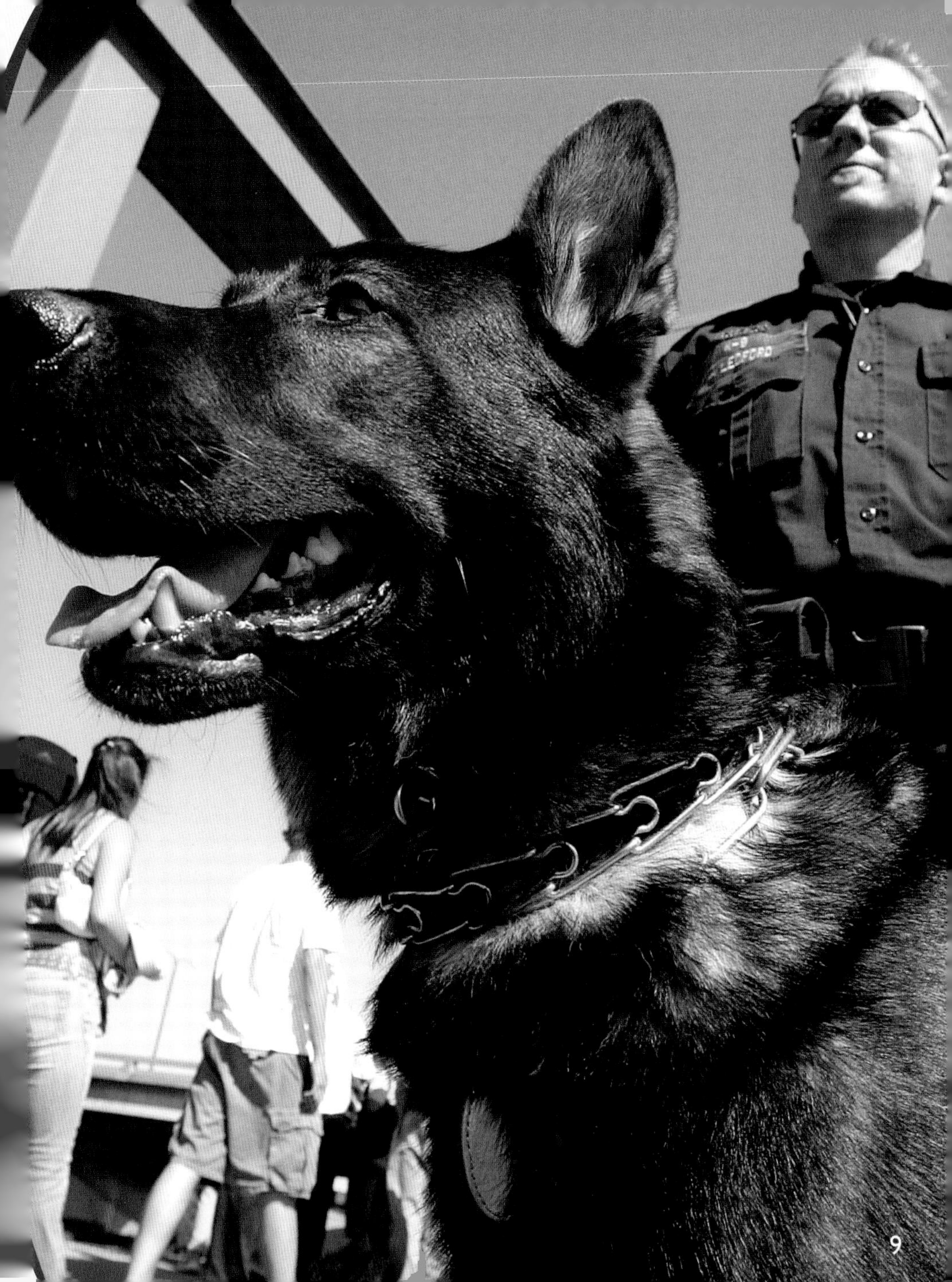

# Horses

This policeman rides a big horse.

The big horse helps the policeman with his job, too.

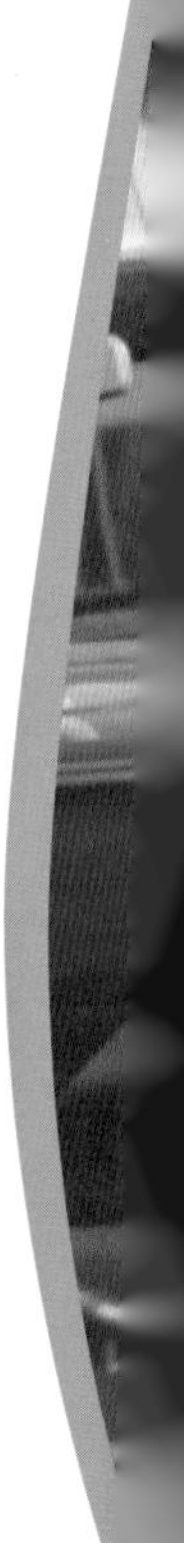

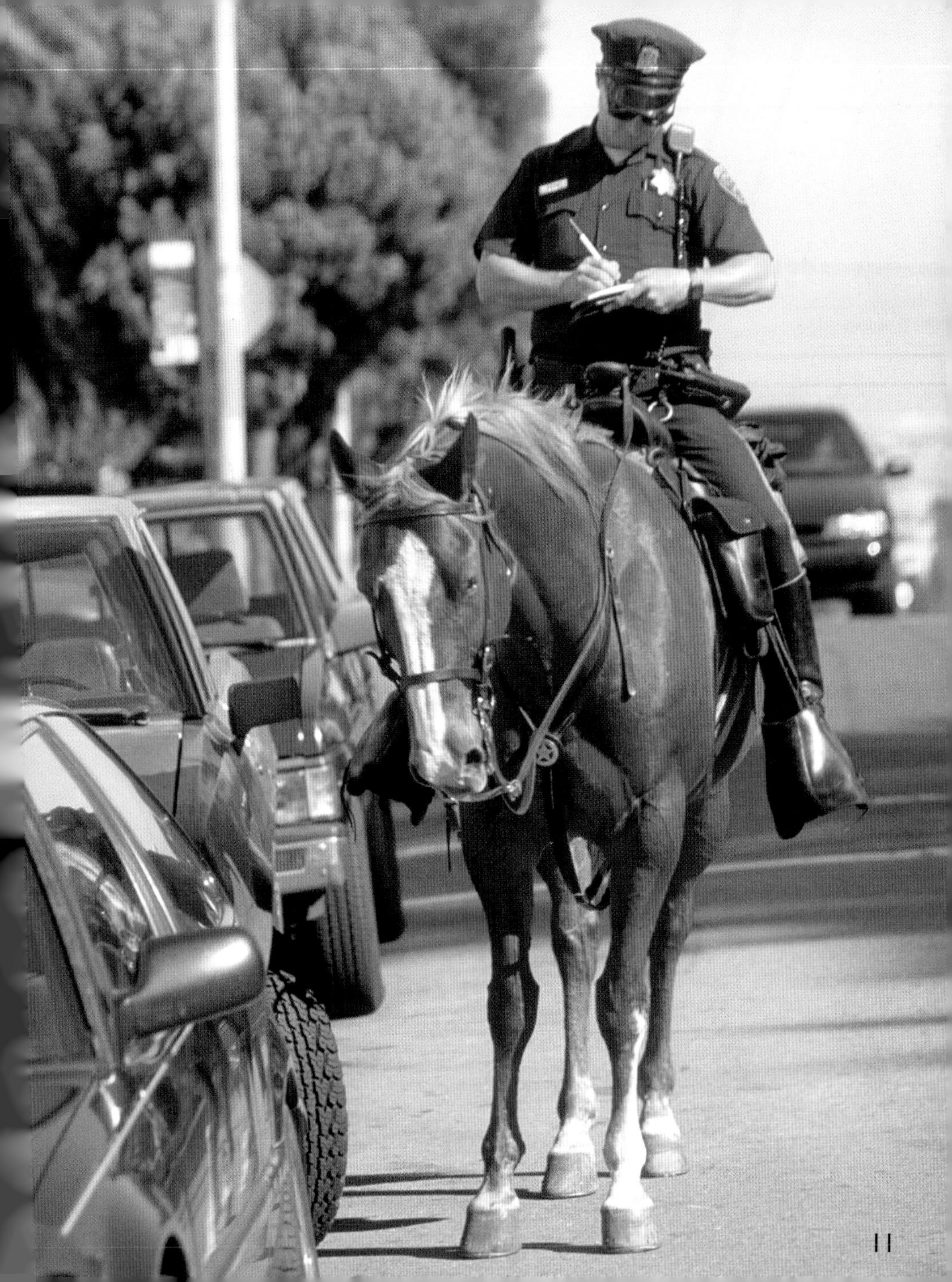

Boys and girls can go
for a ride
on a horse.

When kids ride on
a horse, it helps
them feel safe.

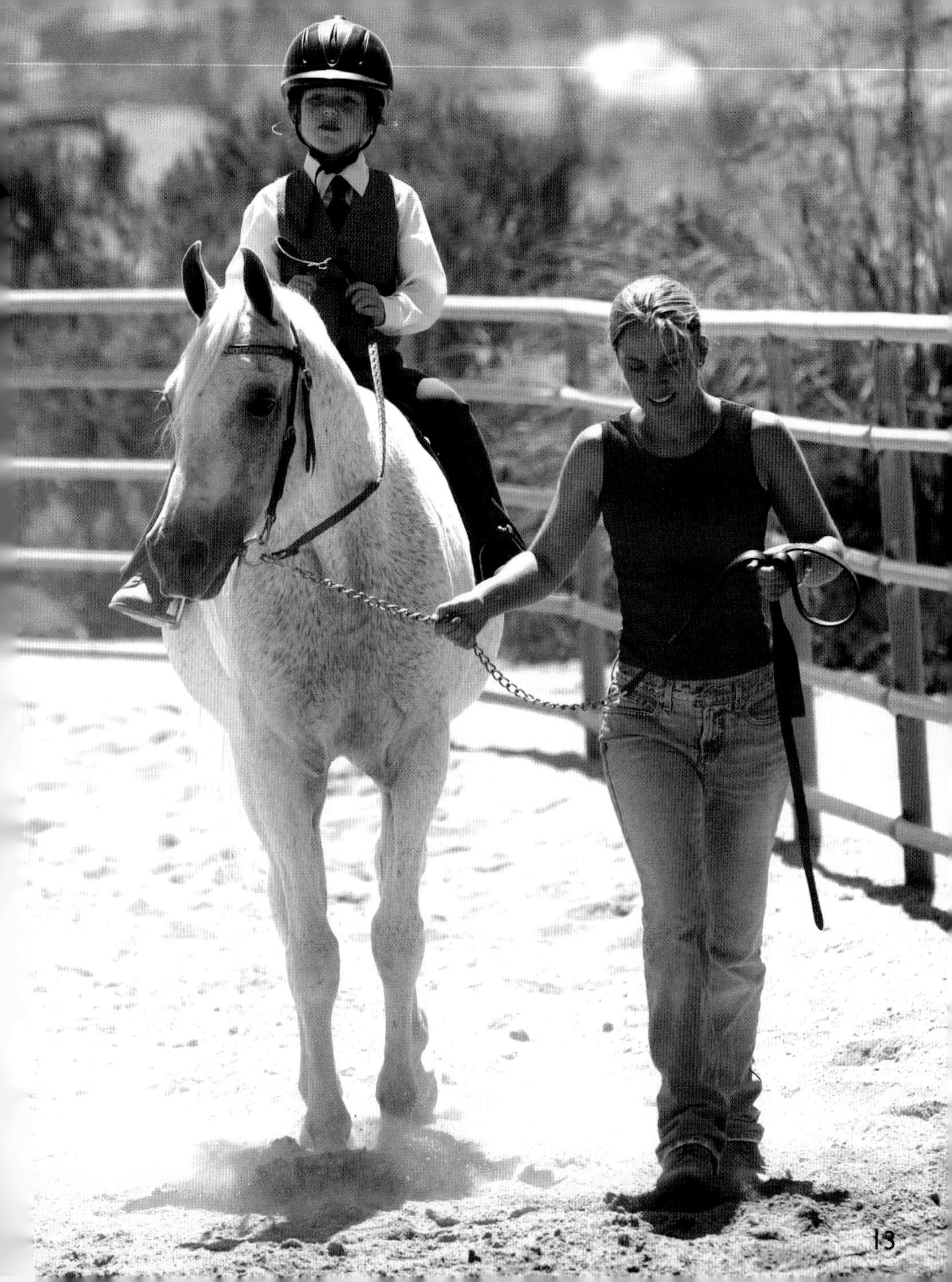

# Elephants

Look at this big elephant.
A man rides the elephant.

The elephant can carry
lots of **logs** for the man.

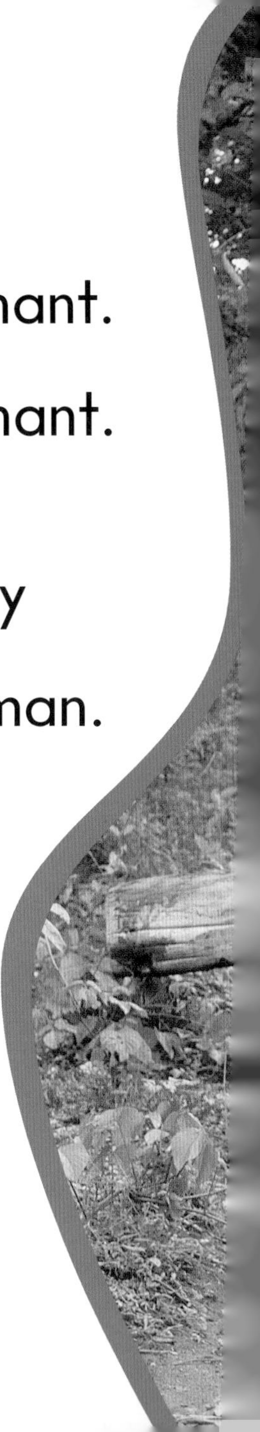

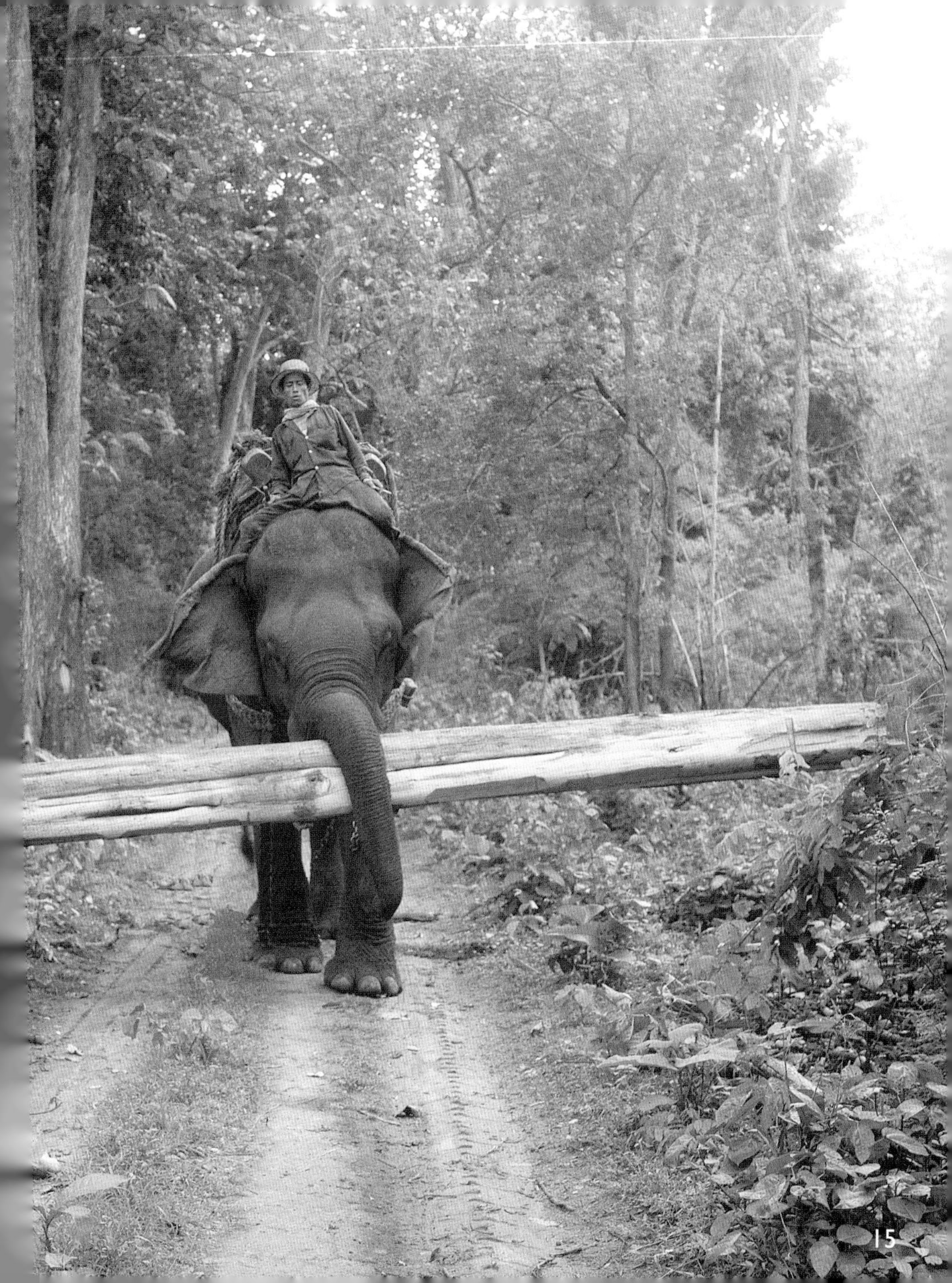

# Glossary

farmer

logs

pet

policeman